Collecting
BURLEIG.

A photographic guide to the Art Deco tablewares of Burgess and Leigh

The first pieces of Burleigh ware purchased by the author. A trio in "Daffodil" on the Zenith shape.

Cover illustrations by Deborah J. Hinks
Front: Pan
Back: Moonbeams

Written and researched by
ELIZABETH R. COUPE

Designed, Typeset and Published by Letterbox Publishing
Unit 1a Rural Industries, John O'Gaunt, Melton Mowbray, Leicestershire LE14 2RE.
Telephone 01664 454114 Fax 01664 454115.

Photographs by Barry Coupe and Claire Coupe or reproduced by kind permission.
Illustrations by Deborah Hinks.

ISBN 09532462 0 5

NOTE: Whilst every care has been taken to ensure the accuracy of the information contained
in this book, the author or publisher cannot accept any responsibility for any omissions or
inaccuracies, or for any loss, direct or consequential, that might be sustained.

Foreword

I *have much pleasure in commending this collectors' guide to the designs which our resident designer, Harold Bennett, produced for Burgess & Leigh in the later 1920's and 1930's. He was a most prolific designer sometimes producing as many as half a dozen sketches in an afternoon. In spite, or perhaps because of this, many of his patterns were of a very high standard and fully in-keeping with the feeling of the time. Elizabeth Coupe, a diligent collector herself, has put together an outstanding collection of his work. This guide covers over 60 patterns and is illustrated by just as many photographs.*

These patterns were produced on three shapes, Zenith a round shape sold with conventional round plates, London a square shape which had its own square plates and Imperial a square hollow shape which was sold with London shape plates and dishes. The Zenith and Imperial shapes were modelled by Ernest Bailey, our very talented young modeller, the London shape, as indicated elsewhere in the guide, by another modeller.

Harold Bennett in addition to his work as a designer was, in his spare time, a well-known local artist, working at first in oils, but after the war in water colour. At that time he had a weekend cottage on the

Staffordshire Moorlands and many of his paintings were of moorland scenes. One of them, a snow scene, after being hung in the Academy, was sold to a well-known firm of Christmas card makers.

I believe that this guide will be most valuable to collectors and enhance the reputation of Harold Bennett's designs.

Edmund Leigh

Chairman - Burgess & Leigh Ltd.

3

About the Author

*A*lthough we have known the author for only a few years, it became immediately apparent that she had a great passion for Art Deco ceramics. Elizabeth's willingness to share her knowledge of ceramics with warmth and conviction is a valuable asset. It is simply this desire to share her love of Burleigh ware with others, that has compelled her to write this guide.

Born in Northallerton, Yorkshire, she moved to Lincoln in 1960 and has remained there ever since. Elizabeth spent some thirty years of her working life teaching, mostly at a local Comprehensive School. She has two daughters and two grandsons and has been married for thirty two years.

Having had a keen interest in ceramics for many years, Elizabeth's hobby led her to begin dealing at the Hemswell Antiques Centres in 1991. Four years later, both she and her husband took early retirement from teaching and now run a successful business.

By producing this colourful insight into the work of Burgess and Leigh, the author hopes to convert you, the reader, into an equally avid follower of their much under-rated ceramics.

KEVIN and JULIE GLOVER

Acknowledgments

I would like to thank the following for their help and support in the production of this guide.

Special thanks are due to Mr Edmund Leigh, the Director of Burgess and Leigh, whose assistance, kindness and personal memories have proved invaluable to me in my research.

Many thanks must also go to my husband, Barry, whose support, patience and photographic skills have been severely tested at times. Thanks, too, to my daughters Deborah and Claire, for their encouragement, illustrations and photography.

My sincere and gratifying thanks also go to Kevin and Julie Glover who have been not only extremely supportive but have helped considerably with the production of this book.

I must give special thanks also to Dave Walsh, who, in response to my initial advertisement, has not only spurred me on but has supplied valuable information and photographs from his own collection.

For their continued help and support, in many forms, I thank my parents, John and Margaret Balch, and friends Tony Hinks and Floyd Varey.

Finally, I would like to thank Pearl Ross-Dale and Julian Gooding for supplying photographs for use within the context of this publication and Richard Bailey for some useful information on certain patterns.

Middleport Pottery

An ariel photograph of the Middleport Pottery as it was in the 1930s.
The seven bottle ovens are clearly shown.
Reproduced from the original by kind permission of Mr Edmund Leigh.

Middleport Pottery

A front view photograph of Burgess and Leigh's Middleport Pottery, situated in Burslem, Stoke-on-Trent.
Opened in 1889, the factory is still in production today.

Former Members of Staff

This group represents some of the members of staff at Burgess and Leigh in 1951, and was taken during the celebrations to commemorate the centenary of the foundation of the firm.

Note that Mr. Edmund Leigh is pictured on the left in front of the door post. Reproduced from the original photograph by kind permission of Mr Edmund Leigh.

Contents

Introduction

*T*he purpose of this Collector's Guide is to make a record of the Art
Deco designs produced for tablewares by Harold Bennett in the
1930's for the firm of Burgess and Leigh – Burleigh Ware. I have
chosen to concentrate solely on the patterns on the Zenith, London and
Imperial shapes, modelled by Ernest Bailey, which form the bulk of my
collection. Sadly, only a few pages of Bennett's pattern books still remain
and these are reproduced with the kind permission of the Leigh family,
who still run the factory.

Many dealers and collectors of Burleigh Ware who have helped me
with this work, agree that these wonderful hand-painted ceramics are
greatly undervalued and that little has been written about them. It is
hoped that, by including as many photographs as possible in this guide,
readers will be able to see and appreciate Bennett's work, considered by
many to be English Art Deco at its finest.

The list of patterns I have included in this guide is by no means
definitive. I realise that there may be many more out there and I would
appreciate any information on these and on the names of patterns which
in some cases have been difficult to find.

Relatively few pieces are back stamped with the pattern name, so
simple descriptions have had to be used. Where this is the case, an
asterisk denotes our own pattern name.

A price guide has also been included but this is just a guide.
Recently prices have risen dramatically, as have those for other 1930's
hand painted wares.

A Brief History of the Factory

The firm of Burgess and Leigh is still being run by the family of William Leigh, one of the founders of the pottery. Edmund Leigh, the present Director, is William's great-grandson and the fourth generation in the family business. William was in partnership with Frederick Burgess.

The pottery's first home was at the Central Pottery, Burslem, but with expansion, soon moved to the Hill Pottery. When this pottery became too small, a new factory was built at Middleport, Burslem, by the side of the Trent and Mersey Canal. The pottery was opened in 1889, and the firm still operates from here, though we believe only one disused bottle oven remains from the original seven, the firing now being done by gas fired kilns.

William Leigh died in 1889 and Frederick Burgess in 1898, so their sons, Edmund and Richard took control of the pottery. When Richard died in 1912, Edmund took over the whole firm and in 1919, when the firm became a Limited Company, Edmund and his three sons became the first directors.

The firm was described before the First World War as a Toilet and General Earthenware Manufacturer and toilet ware accounted for half the output of the factory. In the early 1920's, with the decline in the toilet ware trade, additional tea and dinner wares were introduced. Only a short time later, the fashion for brightly coloured, on glaze decoration developed and this continued throughout the 1930's.

This was a successful and profitable time for Burgess and Leigh. The introduction of the new shapes – Zenith, London and Imperial – of the early 1930's, with their handpainting and enamelling, proved very popular with the public. The new wares were sold in Dinner Sets or Suite ware, which prospective brides could buy in single items for their bottom drawers.

The Second World War with its severe restrictions on productions of all kinds, banned the sale of decorated wares in the

United Kingdom and limited output to "Utility" ranges. Any decorated wares could be exported to alleviate the shortage of foreign money. The Company took advantage of this and still exports a great deal of its production.

In the 1950's, when decorated wares could again be produced, the 1930's methods were too expensive, so lithograph and screen printing transfers were successfully introduced. By the 1960's, contemporary designs were based on the traditional methods of underglaze printing and banding and today the traditional underglaze patterns, Willow, Asiatic Pheasant, Calico etc. form the bulk of the firm's product range which is exported all over the world.

Zenith, London and Imperial

Burgess and Leigh were successful in following the Art Deco trend. Burleigh Ware's designs of the early 1930's had strong sculptural lines and wonderfully handpainted designs.

In about 1930 the Sheraton shape was introduced and this was followed by Zenith, with its straight lines and curves in 1931. (Registration No: 766416). The squarer London shape was first registered in 1932 (Registration No: 772000) and the London Imperial slightly later. The decorations on all these shapes were by Harold Bennett.

The Zenith and Imperial shapes were modelled by Ernest Bailey, who, like Harold Bennett, the Designer, spent the majority of his working life with Burgess and Leigh. He was a local man and it is thought that, along with Bennett, he attended the Burslem School of Art. This cannot be verified, however, as the Stoke on Trent College has no records of students in the first decades of this century.

The London shape was modelled by an outside modeller. It would seem that it was a dinner ware shape only, with plates, meat dishes and vegetable dishes and was sold with Zenith cups and saucers and suite ware until the introduction of the Imperial shape.

Harold Bennett joined the firm at the age of about thirty years, having previously been employed by Gater Hall and Co. He remained as the Art Director and Chief Designer for Burgess and Leigh until his retirement at the age of sixty-five years. Harold Bennett was a wonderful artist with a passion for trees. Having worked all week designing, he spent weekends at his cottage in Staffordshire, painting landscapes. Thanks to information obtained from the Royal Academy, we now know that in 1945, he had two of his works exhibited here. Catalogued as numbers 780 and 964, they were titled "Longsdon, Staffordshire" and "A Moorland Road". At this time it seems that he was living, during the week, at 4 St. George's Avenue, Wolstanton, Staffs. Harold Bennett had one son, Anthony, but I have been unable to trace him. He became a farmer and subsequently ran a restaurant in Market Drayton.

As stated there are only a few of the original pages of Artwork left but the quality of Bennett's work is apparent and we are able to learn a good deal from his pages of patterns. We see that the Zenith shape was produced in Dinner and Suite ware – London in Flat, Imperial and Imperial Suite ware. The Imperial tureens followed the style of the Suite ware, the Flat tureens are some seven inches square and are less ornate, having only a simple moulded square containing a small flower on the handles and cover. Most patterns had a combination of only three or four colours.

London patterns were painted alongside those for the Zenith shape and in some cases the same patterns were used for both, as in the patterns for Brocade and Golden Days. Other patterns were made with London plates and Zenith suite ware.

My own collection contains examples of both "Pan", "Meadowland" and "Primrose" on each shape. We also learn that the basic design was printed on glaze in grey before being hand coloured to Bennett's instructions, the colours of the enamels being listed. Many Burleigh designs are easily recognised by their black dotted edges. It was interesting to learn that these are referred to as 'Sunshine' edges by Bennett, after the first pattern using this treatment. All wares had an ivory glaze. Mr Leigh remembered that "Dawn" on the Zenith shape was one of the most popular designs and that a full dinner service in "Dawn" comprising of 2 vegetable dishes, 2 tureens, a gravy boat, 18 plates and 3 meat plates, cost the grand sum of 35s 4d!

Surprisingly, he believed that Moonbeams was not such a good seller. This could explain its rarity today.

The Suite Ware was produced in the numerous tableware designs, allowing people to collect not only dinner and tea services, but many other items. Tea Sets did not include a teapot, although three sizes of teapots were produced at this time. Coffee Sets, with a coffee pot, six small cups and saucers and a small sugar and cream were also made, as were Morning Sets with a small teapot, two tea cups and saucers and a small sugar and cream also. Additionally there were Sandwich Sets with a rectangular tray and six small plates, and matching fruit sets comprising a bowl and six rimmed fruits, these sets being intended for stewed fruit rather than fresh.

Toast racks, preserve pots, biscuit barrels, salad sets, cruets on stands and egg sets of both five and seven pieces (a tray and four or six footless egg cups) were also produced, as were individual footed egg cups, spoons and ladles. I have a "Meadowland" Egg Set on a stand which comprises four egg cups and a salt and pepper pot. Meal times must have been extremely colourful.

Although both have similar hand painted designs, the London and Zenith shapes were quite different as can be seen from the illustrations. Plates in Zenith are round, whereas the London plates have a squarer appearance with the corners removed, similar to the later Midwinter design. Imperial cups, coffee pots, jugs etc. appear generally squarer, less angular and not as conical in shape as those in Zenith. The moulded leaves and flowers on handles are on the base of the handle on Zenith, but on Imperial they are at the top.

It is truly unfortunate that the main pattern books are lost. By collecting together as many photographs as possible for this guide, perhaps Bennett's wonderful designs may be preserved and recognised by a greater number of people, as being of major importance to English Art Deco ceramics.

A Meadowland Egg Set

Fragrance

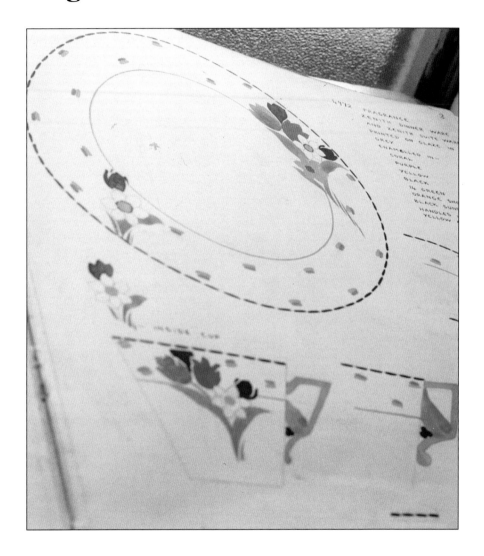

A page from Harold Bennett's original pattern book showing his designs and drawings for Fragrance (Pattern No. 4972) on the Zenith shape in Dinner and Suite ware.

Brocade

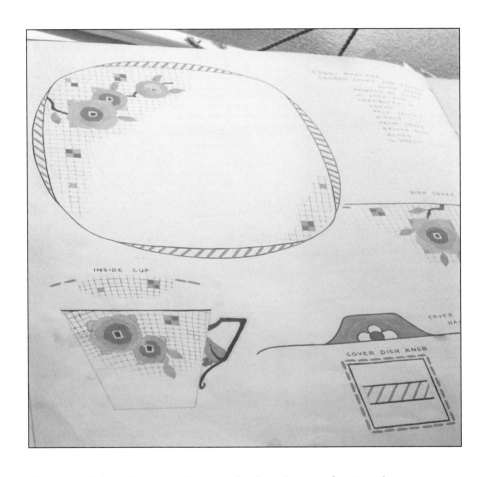

Reproduced from the original pattern book is the page for Brocade
(Pattern No. 5044).
It shows London Flat ware and Zenith Suite ware together.
The plate is London and the cup is Zenith.

Moonbeams (Green)

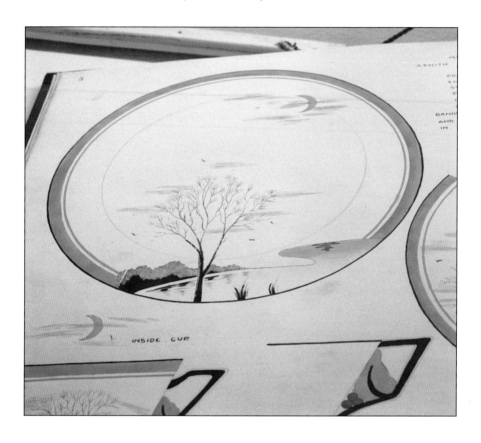

A beautiful Art Deco design on the Zenith shape.
Moonbeams was produced in two colourways.
This shows the Green version (Pattern No. 5046)

Moonbeams (Grey)

The other version of Moonbeams as produced in Grey (Pattern No. 5045).

Golden Days

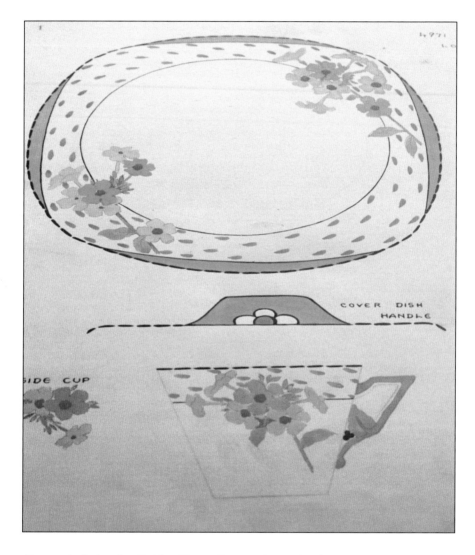

Bennett's design for Golden Days (Pattern No. 4971).
Again London and Zenith shapes appearing side by side.

Riviera

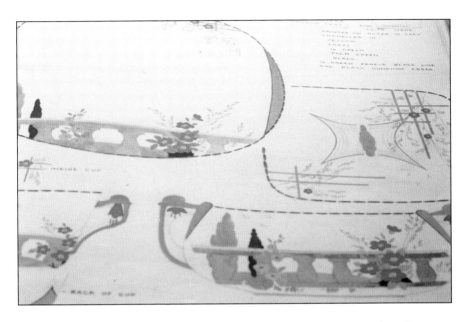

This page of Riviera designs (Pattern No. 5088) gives us examples of Imperial Suite ware as well as London flat. The tureen replicates the tea ware.

A London plate in Riviera pattern.

List of Known Patterns

*Description only (true pattern name unknown)

APPLE TREE*
AUTUMN LEAVES*
BAMBOO*
BARLEY*
BEECHNUT*
BIARRITZ
BLACK SQUARE*
(IN PINK AND GREEN)
BLUEBELL
BLUEBERRY
BLUE DAHLIA*
BLUE PRIMULA*
BOAT*
BOUQUET
BROCADE
BULLRUSH
BUSY LIZZIE*
BUTTERCUP*
BUTTERFLIES*
CORN AND POPPIES*
CORNFLOWER
CROCUS
DAFFODIL
DAWN
DUSK*
EVERGREEN
FIR
FERN*
FLAG IRIS*
FLORETTE
FRAGRANCE
FUCHSIA
GOLDEN DAYS

GRAPES*
GRASSES*
HOLLYHOCKS*
LAKESIDE*
LABURNUM
LEMON TREE*
LILY POND
LUPIN*
MAYTIME
MOONBEAMS
ORANGE DAHLIA*
ORANGE LEAF*
ORANGE LEAF & BERRIES*
ORANGE TREE*
PAN
PANSY
PINK FLOWERS*
POLYANTHUS*
PRIMROSE
REEDS*
RIVIERA
ROSE TREE*
SHIRLEY
SPA
SPINNING WHEEL
SPRING FLOWERS*
SUNRAY
SWEET PEA
TRANQUIL
TRAILING FUCHSIA*
TREE & RED FLOWERS*
TULIP TIME
WILD STRAWBERRY

Meadowland

MEADOWLAND (Pattern No. 4807). A bright pattern of cowslips – with the exception of the cake plate, all items are on Zenith.

A Meadowland
Morning Set,
shown courtesy
of Julian
Gooding.

Dawn

One of Mr Bennett's most successful patterns, Dawn (Pattern No. 4760), depicts a stylised tree and the sun rising.
A toast rack and two unusual dishes are positioned in the front row.
The toast rack supports two trees. All are on the Zenith shape.

Dawn (Breckland)

In the orange colourway Dawn (Pattern No. 4772) is very eyecatching.
All the shapes are in Zenith. The author is not aware of any Dawn pieces on
the London shape.

Primrose

A delicate, restful design, Primrose (Pattern No. 5138) is very English in inspiration, as are many of Bennett's designs.
The plates are London flat, the other pieces are Zenith Suite ware.

Bluebell

Harold Bennett's love of trees is shown to good effect in this attractive Bluebell (Pattern No. 4829) design on the Zenith shape.

Bullrush & Biarritz

Bullrush (Pattern
No. 5353).
The bowl clearly
shows the truncated
conical shape of
Zenith Suite Ware.
Note the omission of
"sunshine" edges.

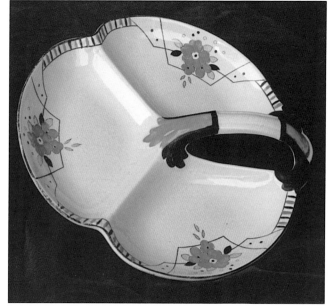

Biarritz
An hors d'oeuvres
dish in the green
and black pattern
of Biarritz.

Pan

A combination of London and Zenith, this Pan (Pattern No. 4827) tea set explores the spirit of Nature. Pan is seen playing his pipes, whilst sitting beneath a tree. Giant mushrooms are seen growing in the foreground. This is possibly the most sought after design.

Daffodil

The owner of this Daffodil (Pattern No. 4813) dinner and suite ware kindly allowed us to reproduce these photographs. Given to her by her mother, they were her mother's engagement and wedding presents in 1935. She is now the proud owner of over 100 pieces of Daffodil.

A Daffodil Sauce Tureen — a rare piece even without the ladle. Courtesy of Pearl Ross-Dale.

Butterflies

(Pattern No. 5080)
This delightful design on London Flat and Imperial is delicately painted with butterflies and meadow grasses.
Few patterns appear to bear insects.

Evergreen

A Coffee Set in Evergreen (Pattern No. 5246) on the London Imperial shape. Courtesy of Dave Walsh.

Maytime

Set in Maytime (Pattern No. 5252) and a sandwich plate
Photographs shown courtesy of Dave Walsh.

Maytime –
An
impressive
biscuit barrel.

Teapot – Moonbeams

(Pattern No. 5045)
A superb teapot in Moonbeams Grey colourway. The photographs showing both front and back designs.
Courtesy of Dave Walsh.

Teapots and Coffee Pots

TEA POTS – Zenith teapots in 3 different sizes and designs.
Left to right: Primrose, Unknown (Tree with Red Flowers) and Dawn.

COFFEE
POTS –
Meadowland
Zenith (left)
and Butterflies
London (right).

Trios

Above: Imperial – Barley. Zenith – Orange Tree
Below: Zenith – Fragrance

Jugs

SIX ZENITH JUGS
Back Left to right: Meadowland, Corn & Poppies, Primrose
Front Left to right: Bluebell, Dawn, Fragrance

LITTLE &
LARGE!
Fragrance
(3-inches high)
Black Square –
Pink
(10.75-inches
in height)

Sugars

Left to Right: Pink Flowers, Tranquil and Tulip Time.
Back: A Rose Tree patterned teapot stand.

FUCHSIA –
Courtesy of
Mr. Edmund
Leigh.

Tureens

*Above: Zenith Tureens – Daffodil, Autumn Leaves, Grasses and
Busy Lizzie.*
Below: Cornflower on a London Imperial Tureen photographed at Newark.

London Flat Tureens

These tureens are much less ornate both in design and decoration.
Above: Lupin (Pattern No. 4054).
Below: Black Square – Green.

Plates in Zenith

The following
six plates are
still in the
possession of
the firm.

Flag Iris

Polyanthus

Wild
Strawberry

Plates in Zenith (continued)

*These photos
are printed
courtesy of Mr.
Edmund Leigh*

Pansy

Spring Flowers

Fern

Plates in Zenith & London

Another selection of Zenith patterns
Back Left to right: Grasses, Laburnum, Bamboo
Front Left to right: Grapes, Fir, Hollyhocks
Below Left: Maytime – Right: Lakeside (both in London)

Plates in London

Above Back Left to right: Trailing Fuchsia, Buttercup
Front Left to right: Florette, Crocus, Lupin
Below Meat plates: Orange Leaf, Reeds, Blue Dahlia (Pattern No. 5067),
Black Square – Green

Fruit Sets – London & Zenith

Above Left to right: Apple Tree, Sunray, Sweet Pea –London
Below: A Zenith Fruit Set in Beechnut

Bouquet

The Bouquet pattern seen on Zenith, but used on this more conventionally shaped Tea Set. Courtesy of Dave Walsh.

Miscellaneous

Lily Pond

Tranquil

Lemon Tree

Shapes – 1

Zenith   ## London Imperial

Teapot.

Teacup.

 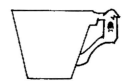

Plate.

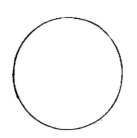 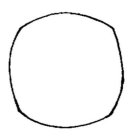

Shapes – 2

Zenith   ## *London Imperial*

Coffee pot.

Jug.

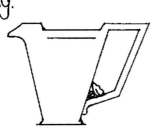

Tureen.

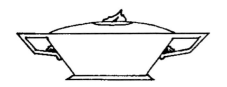

Price Guide

The price guide has been divided into three groups.

GROUP A – Items with minimal decoration and less desirable patterns. e.g. Bullrush.

GROUP B – Popular patterns with bright floral designs. e.g. Meadowland and Daffodil.

GROUP C – Rarer, strong Deco designs on Zenith and London Imperial. e.g. Pan, Moonbeams, Riviera. Please remember, condition is also important.

	GROUP A	GROUP B	GROUP C
TEA SETS	£200–250	£300–350	£400–450
COFFEE SETS	£150–200	£250–300	£300–400
MORNING SETS	£100–150	£200–250	£250–300
TEA POTS			
8-inches	£60–80	£80–100	£100–150
7-inches	£50–70	£70–90	£90–140
6-inches	£40–60	£60–80	£80–120
COFFEE POTS	£40–50	£50–60	£70–100
JUGS			
7-inches	£30–40	£40–60	£60–100
6-inches	£25–35	£35–55	£50–90
5.5-inches	£20–30	£30–50	£45–85
4-inches	£20–25	£25–40	£40–60
3-inches	£15–20	£20–35	£35–50

Price Guide (continued)

	GROUP A	GROUP B	GROUP C
TRIO	£20–30	£35–45	£45–55
COFFEE CUP & SAUCER	£15–25	£25–35	£35–45
SUGAR BOWLS			
4-inches diam.	£15–20	£25–35	£35–45
3-inches diam.	£12–15	£20–30	£30–40
PLATES – including soup, sandwich, cakestands etc.			
18-inches	£30–40	£35–45	£45–50
16-inches	£25–35	£30–35	£40–45
14-inches	£20–25	£20–30	£35–40
12-inches	£15–20	£18–25	£30–35
10-inches	£12–15	£15–20	£25–35
9-inches	£10–12	£12–15	£20–30
7-inches	£8–10	£10–12	£15–20
TUREENS	£20–30	£30–40	£40–60
GRAVY BOAT	£15–20	£20–25	£30–40
TOAST RACKS	£20–25	£30–40	£45–55
BISCUIT BARREL	£50–60	£55–65	£80–100
EGG & CRUET SETS	£45–50	£55–75	£70–100
PRESERVE POTS	£25–35	£35–45	£45–65
FRUIT SETS	£40–50	£50–70	£70–90
SANDWICH SETS	£45–55	£55–65	£70–90
CHEESE DISH	£30–40	£40–60	£80–100

Backstamps

Examples of pictorial backstamps;

Some pieces bear an impressed date mark, often accompanied by the word Ivory, which refers to the glaze.

Conclusion

*B*urgess and Leigh produced many other fine ceramics in the 1930s. Their fancy wares, especially the jugs, for which they are perhaps best known, are keenly collected and highly prized.

They produced vases, wall ornaments, bowls etc. in the Art Deco style and these have been documented elsewhere. I hope that this Photographic Guide has been of some help and will encourage the appreciation of Burleigh's lesser known but equally impressive table-wares.

If anyone is interested in joining a Collectors Club, or has further information or comments concerning this publication, they are more than welcome to contact me via the publisher:

Elizabeth Coupe
c/o Letterbox Publishing
Unit 1a Rural Industries
John O'Gaunt
Melton Mowbray
Leicestershire
LE14 2RE.

Framed prints of the original artwork for the
cover illustrations by Deborah Hinks
may be purchased by sending a cheque for £15.00
made payable to Elizabeth Coupe
(to include postage and packing) to the above address.
Please specify Pan or Moonbeams.

Notes

Hemswell
Antiques Centres

270 Shops in Three Adjacent Buildings
selling

Period Furniture — Shipping Furniture
Pine Furniture
Oriental Rugs — Long Case Clocks
Jewellery — Prints — Books — Silver
Pictures — Ceramics and many Collectables

Tel: Hemswell 668389
(STD 01427)

Open Daily 10.00a.m. to 5.00p.m.

10 Miles North of Lincoln
1 Mile from Caenby Corner
on the A631 to Gainsborough
Newark 25 Miles

Licensed Restaurant

Nationwide Deliveries arranged.
Container, Packing Service.
Single item shipping arranged.
Car Parking for 400 cars.

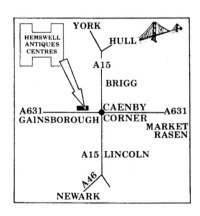

Hemswell Antiques Centres,
Caenby Corner Estate, Hemswell Cliff, Gainsborough, Lincs. DN21 5TJ.